W9-CPE-320

PARTHENON

James De Medeiros

www.av2books.com

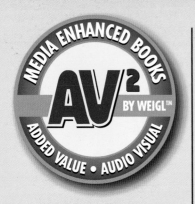

MEDIA ENHANCED BOOKS
AV²
BY WEIGL™
ADDED VALUE • AUDIO VISUAL

AV² provides enriched content that supplements and complements this book. Weigl's AV² books strive to create inspired learning and engage young minds in a total learning experience.

Your AV² Media Enhanced books come alive with...

Audio
Listen to sections of the book read aloud.

Key Words
Study vocabulary, and complete a matching word activity.

Video
Watch informative video clips.

Quizzes
Test your knowledge.

Embedded Weblinks
Gain additional information for research.

Slide Show
View images and captions, and prepare a presentation.

Try This!
Complete activities and hands-on experiments.

... and much, much more!

Go to **www.av2books.com**, and enter this book's unique code.

BOOK CODE

Q466158

AV² by Weigl brings you media enhanced books that support active learning.

Published by AV² by Weigl
350 5th Avenue, 59th Floor
New York, NY 10118

Website: www.av2books.com www.weigl.com

Library of Congress Cataloging-in-Publication Data

De Medeiros, James.
 Parthenon / James De Medeiros
    p. cm. -- (Virtual field trips)
 ISBN 978-1-61690-768-6 (hardcover : alk. paper) -- ISBN 978-1-61690-772-3 (paperback : alk. paper) -- ISBN 978-1-61690-434-0 (online)
 1. Parthenon (Athens, Greece)--Juvenile literature. 2. Athens (Greece)--Buildings, structures, etc.--Juvenile literature. I. Title.
 NA281.K57 2011
 726'.120809385--dc23
                     2011019313

Printed in the United States of America in North Mankato, Minnesota
2 3 4 5 6 7 8 9 0 15 14 13 12 11

092011
WEP230911

Editor: Heather Kissock
Design: Terry Paulhus

Every reasonable effort has been made to trace ownership and to obtain permission to reprint copyright material. The publishers would be pleased to have any errors or omissions brought to their attention so that they may be corrected in subsequent printings.

Weigl acknowledges Getty Images as its primary image supplier for this title.

Contents

What is the Parthenon?

A visit to Greece would not be complete without a stroll through the ruins of the Parthenon. Located on a hill high above the city of Athens, the Parthenon is a rectangular building with tall, white columns. At one time, the building served as the temple of the **Acropolis**. Inside the Parthenon, the Greeks stored **treasury** funds, gifts, and a statue of Athena, the goddess of war and wisdom.

The Parthenon was built at the instruction of Pericles, a powerful political leader in Athens during the period of 447–432 BC. At this time, Athens was experiencing great prosperity, and the decision was made to build the Parthenon in honor of the goddess Athena. A previous attempt to build a temple in honor of the goddess had been burned by the Persians, who attacked Greece in 480 BC.

Pericles chose Ictinus to be the primary **architect** responsible for building the Parthenon. Another architect called Kallikrates was hired to help Ictinus with the building's construction. Phidias, a **sculptor**, was assigned the job of designing the statue of Athena.

While the Parthenon is no longer a place of worship or a treasury, it is difficult to imagine Greece without this spectacular structure. More than four million people come to see it every year.

The Parthenon is considered to be the most important building from Ancient Greece that still exists today. Its sculptures are a testament to the artistry of the time.

Snapshot of Greece

Greece is located in southern Europe at the southern end of the Balkan Peninsula. It shares its northern border with Bulgaria, Macedonia, Albania, and Turkey. The rest of the country is surrounded by water. The Mediterranean Sea lies to its south, the Ionian Sea to its west, and the Aegean Sea to its East.

INTRODUCING GREECE

CAPITAL CITY: Athens

FLAG:

POPULATION: 11,306,183 (2010)

OFFICIAL LANGUAGE: Greek

CURRENCY: Euro

CLIMATE: Mediterranean, with mild temperatures, plenty of sunshine, and moderate rainfall

SUMMER TEMPERATURE: 66° to 82° Fahrenheit (19° to 28° Celsius)

WINTER TEMPERATURE: 50° to 59° F (10° to 15° C)

TIME ZONE: Eastern European Time (EET)

THE FORMER YUGOSLAV REPUBLIC OF MACEDONIA

BULGARIA

ALBANIA

TURKEY

GREECE

Aegean Sea

★ Athens

Ionian Sea

Sea of Crete

Greece

------- International Boundary

★ National Capital

N

0   50   100 Kilometers
0   50   100 Miles

Mediterranean Sea

Greek Words to Know

When visiting a foreign country, it is always a good idea to know some words and phrases of the local language. Practice the phrases below to prepare for a trip to Greece.

pah-rah-kah-LOH
Please/You're welcome/Excuse me?

YAH-su
Hello/Goodbye

eff-kha-rees-TOH
Thank you

mee-LAHS Ang-lee-KAH
Do you speak English?

Neh
Yes

poh-soh KAH-nee
How much is it?

meh LEH-neh
My name is

seegh-NO-mee
Sorry

boh-REE-teh nah
Can you help me?

Oh-hee
No

tee-KAH-nis
How are you?

POHS seh LEH-neh
What is your name?

A Step Back In Time

From 480 to 479 BC, the Persians invaded and burnt the temples on the Acropolis. In 447, Pericles decided that, since Athens was enjoying such great prosperity, the time had come to restore the Acropolis to its former state. Pericles' plan was to build the Parthenon on the exact same place as the previous temple that had been destroyed by the Persians. His idea was to make the Parthenon the most amazing shrine to the goddess Athena. When finished, the Parthenon was a beautiful structure made entirely with marble from Mount Pentelicus, which is about 10 miles (16 kilometers) away from Athens.

CONSTRUCTION TIMELINE

489 to 480 BC
Themistocles starts the construction of the first Parthenon.

480 to 479 BC
The Persians invade Athens and burn the temples of the Acropolis, including the original Parthenon.

479 to 449 BC
The decision is made to make Athens a strong city both politically and economically. Rebuilding the temple is not a priority, however.

449 BC
Pericles decides to rebuild the temple at the Acropolis.

447 to 432 BC
Pericles hires Ictinus, Kallikrates, and Phidias to work on the construction of the new Parthenon. It is completed in 432 BC.

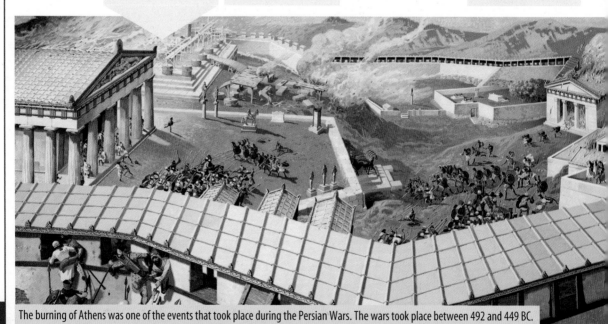

The burning of Athens was one of the events that took place during the Persian Wars. The wars took place between 492 and 449 BC.

Many of Pericles' political enemies did not like the way the structure was built. They felt that too much of the public's funds were spent on the building. The total cost of the structure is not known. However, the Parthenon cost more to build than any other temple in Greece at that time. It took many years to pay for the project.

The Parthenon remained a shrine to Athena until the sixth century.

Circa AD 500
The Greeks begin using the Parthenon as a **Christian** church. It remains a church for nearly 900 years.

AD 1460
The Turks invade Greece. Under Turkish rule, the Parthenon becomes a **mosque**.

AD 1687
The Venetians attack the Parthenon and shoot a cannonball at the center of the building. This destroys the middle portion of the structure.

AD 1700s
Some of the sculptures inside the Parthenon are sold to tourists from western Europe.

AD 1801
British ambassador Lord Elgin receives permission from the Turkish Sultan to take sculptures from the building. These sculptures, called the Elgin Marbles, are put on display at the British Museum in London, England. More than 200 years later, the Greek government continues to ask for the pieces to be returned to Greece.

The Elgin Marbles were removed from the Parthenon over a period of 11 years, from 1801 to 1812. About half of the building's sculptures were taken to London.

The Parthenon Location

The Acropolis has towered above the city of Athens for thousands of years. The word acropolis means "upper city." In Ancient Greece, people often constructed their most important buildings on hills. The people lived in the area below and around the hill.

As it was separated from the rest of the community, the Acropolis was considered to be the most secure place in the city. If the city was under attack, the Acropolis served as a refuge for its people. Its position protected important city holdings as well. Many of these holdings, such as the treasury, were found in the Parthenon.

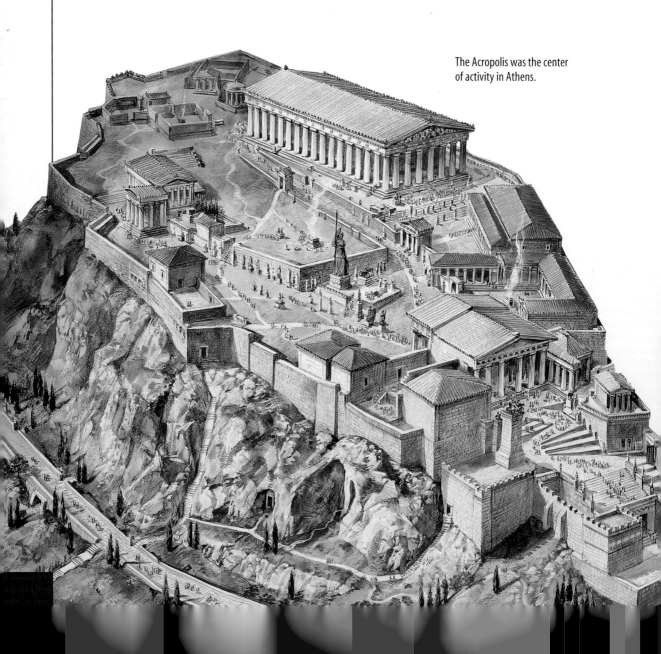

The Acropolis was the center
of activity in Athens.

The Parthenon Today

Today, the Acropolis stands as a testament to Ancient Greece. The buildings are now in ruins, but they still stand majestically above Athens. The most prominent building remains the Parthenon. Its frame of columns and sheer size refer back to a time of grandeur and power.

Columns Modern estimates suggest that a single Parthenon column weighed between 63 and 119 tons (57 and 108 tonnes). Each column has a **diameter** of 6.5 feet.

Height The height of the Parthenon at completion in 432 BC was 65 feet (20 m).

65 feet

6.5 feet

228 feet

101.4 feet

Area The Parthenon was built on the top step of a rectangular platform. The Parthenon is 228.1 feet (70 m) long and 101.4 feet (31 m) wide.

Outside the Parthenon

Greek temples were built to be viewed from the outside. Very few people went inside the temples. Instead, they looked through open doors to get a glimpse of the treasures inside. The outside of the Parthenon had many features that made it interesting to view.

Structure The Parthenon was built on a platform. Forty-six columns run around the perimeter of the structure. At one time, they supported a marble roof. A six-column porch sits at each end of the structure. The porches support triangular areas called pediments.

The Parthenon took more than 15 years to build. It remains standing after more than 2,500 years.

The vertical ridges that run up a Doric column are called fluting.

Columns Most of the Parthenon's columns were created in a style called Doric. The shaft of a Doric column has carved ridges called flutes that run vertically from one end to the other. At the top of the shaft is a plain disk, which has a solid block on top of it. Most Doric columns do not have a base. They sit directly on the structure's platform.

The stylobate has two layers underneath it. These three layers make up the platform.

Platform The Parthenon sits on top of the **stylobate**. This is the top step of the crepidoma, or platform. The top step forms the floor of the Parthenon.

The triglyphs are placed at equal distances apart around the Parthenon.

Triglyph A triglyph sits on each side of a metope. It is a decorative tablet that has two, vertical grooves running through it. These grooves divide the tablet into three parts. It is believed that the pattern represents wooden beams.

When built, the outside of the Parthenon featured 92 metopes. Many of them have since been removed and placed in museums.

Metopes A series of marble panels, called metopes, run along the outside of the Parthenon's walls. The metopes contain sculptures. Each panel displays a scene in which order and justice struggle with criminal elements.

Sculptures Sculptures adorn many parts of the Parthenon. Most tell a story or relate an important historical event. The sculpture on the east pediment shows the birth of the goddess Athena. The sculpture on the west pediment depicts Athena's battle with the god Poseidon for control of Athens. It was a battle Athena won.

VIRTUAL TOUR

The Acropolis is open from 8:00 am to 8:00 pm every day throughout the summer. In the winter, it closes at 3:00 pm. To avoid the intense heat of day, early morning and late afternoon are considered the best times to visit the site.

Greek gods and goddesses, including Demeter and Iris, were featured in many of the Parthenon's sculptures.

Inside the Parthenon

The Parthenon contained two chambers. One room was built to house a statue of Athena. The other, smaller room housed the treasury.

Color While the Parthenon is now white, it was quite colorful when it was first built. Scientists have found traces of green, red, and blue paint on the building's sculptures. The internal ceiling appears to have once been deep blue.

Traces of paint can still be seen on parts of the Parthenon that have not been exposed to weather and sunlight.

Frieze Inside the external columns are the outer walls of the building. A **frieze** runs along the top of these outer walls. The frieze is 1.09 yards (1 m) high and 175 yards (160 m) long. Its sculptures depict the people of Athens in a procession that ends at the Parthenon's entrance. It is believed that the sculpture represents a traditional celebration that was held in honour of the goddess Athena.

About 80 percent of the frieze survives. Most pieces are found in the British Museum as part of the Elgin Marbles.

Treasury The treasury sat behind the statue of Athena. It is in this room that gifts to the goddess were kept. Four **Ionic** columns supported the roof of the treasury. Ionic columns are more decorative than Doric columns. They feature two scrolls at the top.

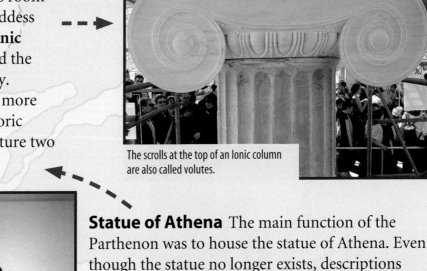

The scrolls at the top of an Ionic column are also called volutes.

Several artists have created their own version of the Statue of Athena. Most of these models are much smaller than the original would have been.

Statue of Athena The main function of the Parthenon was to house the statue of Athena. Even though the statue no longer exists, descriptions of it have been passed down through generations. The statue stood almost 39 feet (12 m) high and was made of gold and ivory. It showed the goddess standing. She wore a tunic, **aegis**, and helmet. Her right hand was extended and held Nike, the goddess of victory. Her left hand held a spear.

Naos The naos was the larger of the two chambers inside the Parthenon. It was here that the statue of Athena was kept. Twenty-three, double-stacked, Doric columns surrounded the statue. A pool of water rested on the floor in front of it, making for a brilliant reflection when light shone in through the Parthenon's entrance.

Long rows of columns, such as those once found in the naos, are called colonnades.

Big Ideas Behind the Parthenon

Ictinus' passion for mathematics is shown in all of his structures. His use of ratios and Doric refinements demonstrate his understanding of the elements needed to build a structure that would be visually appealing and last for a long time.

The Greeks considered the 4:9 ratio to be the most pleasing to the eye. Many of their buildings have been constructed using this ratio.

Ratios

Ratios measure the size of two things in relation to each other. They show how many times one can be contained by the other. When building the Parthenon, Ictinus used the 4:9 ratio to determine measurements of length, width, height, and diameter. Therefore, the length of the temple was slightly more than twice its width. Likewise, the distance between the columns was slightly more than the diameter of the columns. It was believed that using this ratio gave the structure a harmonious appearance.

Doric Refinements

When the Parthenon was built, its columns curved outward in the middle. Ictinus did this to overcome an **optical illusion**. From far away, a vertical straight line is seen as slightly slanted. The curves were planned so that the building would look straight when it was seen in the distance. These line adjustments are called Doric refinements. They made the building look as though it only had straight lines, when it really had none. The upper portions of the columns lean inward as well, helping to create the appearance of straight lines.

Besides curving the columns, the columns were also placed so that they tilted inward. This, too, helped them look straight from a distance.

Science at Work in the Parthenon

Building any kind of structure requires three basic elements—planning, technology, and physical labor. As the chief architect, Ictinus made most of the planning decisions. This included not only the design of the Parthenon, but the materials and construction methods as well.

Marble was chosen to build the Parthenon because it could be easily cut. This allowed it to be used in a variety of ways, from columns to floor tiles.

The Properties of Marble

Marble was used to construct the Parthenon. More than 20,000 tons (18,000 tonnes) of marble were taken from Mount Pentelicus, one of the few places in the world where it can be found in great quality and quantity. Marble is a soft rock. This means that it can be cut and shaped easily. The measurement of hardness scale (MOHS) determines the hardness of a stone based on how easily it can be scratched by grit or hard objects. On this scale, marble is a 3 out of 10. Marble's softness allowed the rock on the Parthenon to be sculpted into beautiful artistic shapes by creating grooves and straight edges.

Simple Machines

Workers relied on simple machines to construct the Parthenon. Due to the weight of the marble, most pieces were sculpted into shape before they left the **quarry**. Sculptors used picks and chisels to cut the marble. Picks and chisels are a type of simple machine called a wedge. A wedge is used to push things apart by converting motion on one end into a splitting motion at the other end. After the marble was cut, it was taken to Athens by wagon. Wagons use a simple machine called a wheel and axle to move objects across distances. Once the marble

Pulleys continue to be used at the Parthenon. Now, they are helping with repairs being made to the site.

arrived at the construction site, workers used another simple machine, the pulley, to lift the marble and put it into place.

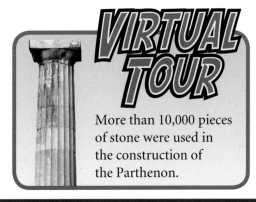

VIRTUAL TOUR

More than 10,000 pieces of stone were used in the construction of the Parthenon.

The Parthenon Builders

Ictinus may have been the main architect on the Parthenon, but there were many others involved in building the structure. Among them were sculptors, carpenters, and quarry workers.

The Temple of Apollo is believed to have been started around 420 BC and completed around 410 BC. It was built for Apollo, the god of healing and the Sun.

Ictinus Chief Architect

The Athenians chose Ictinus to lead the Parthenon's design team because of his outstanding abilities as an architect. Ictinus worked on many temples in Greece, including the Temple of Apollo at Bassai in Arcadia, Peloponnese.

Ictinus is responsible for the incomplete Telesterion at Eleusis, Greece. The Persians destroyed this building, and another one was built when Athens began experiencing economic growth. Ictinus' Telesterion had a smaller number of interior supports than the finished version. These supports were strategically placed around the central shrine. By planning the structure this way, Ictinus was trying to lengthen the building over a larger distance. In doing so, he created the first centrally designed room. This was an idea that he used during the construction of the back room of the Parthenon.

Kallikrates
Secondary Architect

The Temple of Athena Nike was the first temple at the Acropolis to be built in the Ionic style.

The Parthenon's secondary architect was Kallikrates. Kallikrates was the architect for the Temple of Athena Nike, which is also located at the Acropolis. From the stylobate to the top of the structure, the temple is only 11 feet (3.4 meters) tall. The Temple of Athena Nike features four columns on each end of the structure.

Phidias Chief Sculptor

Phidias supervised all of the artistic works created for the Parthenon. His works are known for their grandeur, patriotism, dignity, and proportion. Phidias' work in the Parthenon uses the Golden Ratio. This ratio is based on the idea that rectangles with a length to width ratio of about 1:1.6 are most pleasing to the eye. The basic rule is that the length is always 1.6 times greater than the width. In the Parthenon, the spaces between the columns all form golden rectangles.

Phidias supervised the production of what are now known as the Elgin Marbles.

Carpenters

Carpenters are skilled at working with wood. They craft it to the size and shape needed to make a structure.

Carpenters played an important role in the construction of the Parthenon. Each of the drums of the columns was joined by a wooden fastener. After a notch had been cut into the center of the drum, a carpenter would place a plug inside. Then, using an auger, or hand drill, the carpenter would make a hole in the plug. A circular, wooden pin was placed upright inside the hole. This pin would hold the drum in place when it was stacked as part of a column.

Quarry Workers

Quarry workers used mallets and chisels to take stone from Mount Pentelicus. First, they cut grooves into the marble. Then, they hammered wooden wedges into the grooves and soaked them with water. As the grooves expanded, they would crack the marble. Using crowbars, the quarry workers pried the marble from the mountainside.

Mallets and chisels are still used to cut and shape rock.

Sculptors

Sculptors have played an important role in restoring pieces of the Parthenon, including columns.

Sculptors are artistic people who mold objects from a variety of materials, including marble and bronze. They decide on the materials that they would like to use and then make a sketch of the finished project they hope to create. After completing the rough sketch, they take the materials and begin working on them with a variety of tools. In Ancient Greece, the tools were basic, such as a hammer that could strike a fine edge.

Similar Structures Around the World

The Parthenon is considered by many to be one of the most important and unique structures ever built. Its innovative design and historical significance have influenced the building of many structures around the world.

Federal Hall

BUILT: 1842
LOCATION: New York City, New York
DESIGN: Ithiel Town, Alexander Jackson Davis, John Frazee
DESCRIPTION: Federal Hall uses Doric columns similar to those of the Parthenon. The building was the first Customs House in the United States. Today, it is a National Historic Site that is used as a museum.

The British Museum's original building had four wings. The museum has since expanded in size in order to accommodate its many acquisitions.

The British Museum

BUILT: 1847
LOCATION: London, England
DESIGN: Robert Smirke
DESCRIPTION: The British Museum is an art and historical museum. The Elgin Marbles, originally taken from the Parthenon, are on display at the museum, which was built using stone and includes a copper-domed reading room.

George Washington took the oath of office at Federal Hall. In doing so, he became the first president of the United States.

The Parthenon

BUILT: 1897
LOCATION: Nashville, Tennessee, United States
DESIGN: William C. Smith
DESCRIPTION: Nashville's Parthenon is, in many ways, a tribute to the original. The building and its 42-foot (13-m) statue of Athena are full-scale replicas of the actual Parthenon. It was originally built for Tennessee's Centennial Exposition in 1897 and is currently an art museum.

The Nashville Parthenon was built from brick, stone, and concrete.

More than 120 ceremonies of remembrance are held at the shrine each year.

Shrine of Remembrance

BUILT: 1934
LOCATION: Melbourne, Australia
DESIGN: Peter Hudson and James Wardrop
DESCRIPTION: The Shrine of Remembrance was built as a tribute to the men and women who served during wartime. Hudson and Wardrop won a competition to determine which design would be used for the Shrine of Remembrance. It is considered a Doric architectural design.

Issues Facing the Parthenon

At the time the Parthenon was built, there was not much discussion about the environment. People did not worry about the effects the Parthenon's construction had on the surrounding area. They simply took what they needed and built where they wanted to build.

  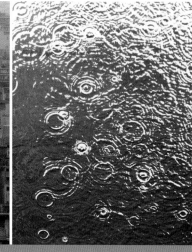

WHAT IS THE ISSUE?

Bird droppings, fungi, and plant roots are reacting with the marble of the structure, resulting in erosion.	Due to the humidity in Greece, moisture stays in the air for a long time. Slowly evaporating water is causing electrochemical damage.	**Acid rain** is causing chemical damage to the Parthenon in the form of corrosion.

EFFECTS

Erosion causes the marble of the Parthenon to become worn down and dirty.	The water is causing the surface of the Parthenon's marble exterior to turn into gypsum, or hydrated calcium sulphate. The result is that much of the Parthenon's marble is wearing down.	Black crusts have formed on the inward-facing portions of the columns. Sulfuric acid in the crusts is eating away at the marble.

ACTION NEEDED

The Parthenon must be cleaned regularly to prevent further damage.	The Parthenon is undergoing reconstruction. Some marble pieces are being removed from the site and displayed in the Parthenon museum. Other marble is being replaced.	Laser technology is being used to clean the marble and remove the black crusts.

Make a Golden Rectangle

Ictinus had a deep appreciation for math and science. He was one of the first people to use ratios in developing architectural designs. One of the ratios connected with the Parthenon is the Golden Rectangle. The Golden Rectangle is a ratio that is always 1:1.6. No matter how many times the point where two sides connect is moved, the ratio remains the same.

Try this activity to explore the concept of the Golden Rectangle.

Materials
- a sheet of paper
- ruler
- pencil
- scissors

Instructions
1. Draw a rectangle on the sheet of paper, with the width being 6.5 inches (16.5 centimeters) and the length being 10.5 inches (27 cm).

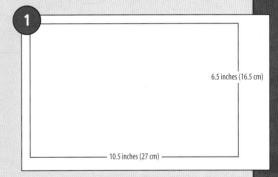

2. Divide the length by the width. Your answer should be 1.6.

3. Use the pencil to draw a square inside the rectangle. The outer edge of the rectangle should make up one side of the square. Each side of the square should be 6.5 inches (16.5 cm), equal to the width of the rectangle.

4. Using the scissors, cut the square out of the page.

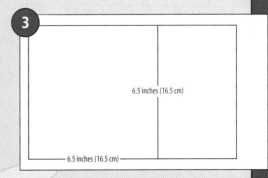

5. With the ruler, take the measurements of the remaining rectangle, and convert any fractions into decimals. To convert fractions into decimals, divide the top number by the bottom number.

6. Divide the length by the width. The result will once again be 1.6, as it was with the original example.

Parthenon Quiz

Q What are three main forms of environmental damage to the Parthenon?

A The three main forms of environmental damage are erosion, electrochemical, and corrosion.

Q What building ratio was used throughout the Parthenon?

A The 4:9 ratio (length: width) was used on the Parthenon.

Q Why were no straight lines used on the Parthenon?

A There are no straight lines on the Parthenon because vertical straight lines are seen as slightly slanted to the unaided eye.

Q How many tons of marble were used to build the Parthenon?

A More than 20,000 tons (18,000 tonnes) of marble were used.

Glossary

acid rain: the result of a chemical transformation which occurs after sulfur dioxide and nitrogen oxides are emitted into the air and absorbed by water droplets in the clouds

Acropolis: the fortified part of a Greek city

aegis: a shield or breastplate

architect: a person who designs buildings

Christian: a person who believes in and follows the teachings of Jesus Christ

diameter: the length of a line that passes through the center of a circle from one side to the other

frieze: a decoration or series of decorations forming an ornamental band around a room

Ionic: a style of columns that is curved to make the column visually appealing

mosque: a Muslim place of worship

optical illusion: something that appears to be different from what it actually is

quarry: a place where stone is dug out for use in a building or sculpture

sculptor: a person who makes statues and other figures out of rock and other materials

stylobate: a horizontal column of rock that supports a vertical column

treasury: a place for storing money and other valuable items

Index

Log on to www.av2books.com

AV² by Weigl brings you media enhanced books that support active learning. Go to www.av2books.com, and enter the special code found on page 2 of this book. You will gain access to enriched and enhanced content that supplements and complements this book. Content includes video, audio, web links, quizzes, a slide show, and activities.

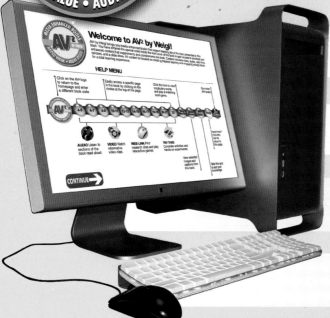

Audio
Listen to sections of the book read aloud.

Video
Watch informative video clips.

Embedded Weblinks
Gain additional information for research.

Try This!
Complete activities and hands-on experiments.

WHAT'S ONLINE?

Try This!	Embedded Weblinks	Video	EXTRA FEATURES
Test your knowledge of Greek. Test your knowledge of the history of the Parthenon in a timeline activity. Learn more about the math behind the Parthenon. Compare modern architects with ancient ones. Write about an issue in your community that is similar to one facing the Parthenon. Complete a fun, interactive activity about the Parthenon.	Find out more about where the Parthenon is located. Learn more about a notable person from the history of the Parthenon. Learn more about becoming an architect. Find out more about other important structures near the Parthenon.	Watch a video introduction to the Parthenon. Watch a video about another tour destination near the Parthenon.	**Audio** Listen to sections of the book read aloud. **Key Words** Study vocabulary, and complete a matching word activity. **Slide Show** View images and captions and prepare a presentation **Quizzes** Test your knowledge.

AV² was built to bridge the gap between print and digital. We encourage you to tell us what you like and what you want to see in the future.

Sign up to be an AV² Ambassador at www.av2books.com/ambassador.